Star and Sparrow Rest

John McGuckian

SUMMER PALACE PRESS

First published in 2008 by

Summer Palace Press
Cladnageeragh, Kilbeg, Kilcar, County Donegal, Ireland

© John McGuckian, 2008

Printed by Nicholson & Bass Ltd.

A catalogue record for this book is available
from the British Library

ISBN 978-0-9560995-1-8

This book is printed on elemental chlorine-free paper

for Mary

Acknowledgments

Some of the poems in this book have previously appeared in: *The Cork Literary Review*; *HU*; and in the anthology *The Blackbird's Nest* (Blackstaff, 2006). Some have been published by the Spanish Academy for English and American Studies and by Louisiana State University.

We wish to thank Pat McKay, Place Names, Queen's University, Belfast and Jill, Department of Spanish, Queen's University, Belfast.

Biographical Note

John McGuckian was born in Ballymena, County Antrim. At the Queen's University, Belfast, he studied geography under the inspiration of Estyn Evans, and was a Full Blue in Association Football. He is a recent MA graduate of the Seamus Heaney Centre for Poetry in Belfast. He has read at the International Poetry Festival, Visby, Sweden; at the John Hewitt Spring School, Carnlough, and at the Summer School of the Seamus Heaney Centre. His first collection, *Talking with My Brother*, was published in 2002.

CONTENTS

Old Pro	11
Braid Valley Morn	12
Hansel	13
Mistle	15
Hallo, Seághan!	16
Caugherty FC	19
Doin' the Ton	22
N. Antrim	23
Lough Money	24
Ain Toun Bully	25
Marengo	26
Permaculture: Antrim Style	27
Missing Persons	30
The Layde, Ballymena	32
Braid Sheddings	
The Potato Harvest	34
The Potato Inspector	36
Peeling Potatoes	37
Brother	38
De Natura Rerum	39
Paying What They Ask	40
Headstones	41

The Home Chapel	42
2002?	43
First Class	44
The Starry Plough	45
Across Such Great Divide	49
Midlands	50
The Last Pair of Wolves	
Aughnabrack, 1692	51
Alone	52
Breath Across the Braid	53
White Rainbow	55
The Effect of Lightning	56
Gonzalo de Cordoba – The Great Captain	58
Matamoros	59
The Tao of Pooh	61
Geography Lessons	
Ballymena Technical College, 1968	63
St Patrick's College, 1982	63
Ballymena Sky	64

Old Pro

Just before he left this world
He played a little tune
On his tin whistle

To the waves at Tornaroan
To our hearts
Along the Antrim shore

Just before he left this world
For to draw my tears
Like a child

From his inside pocket
His very heart
A last request

The Snowy-Breasted Pearl
I said, fighting within myself
To let my brother go.

Braid Valley Morn
for my sisters

Oh we remember –
Watch these beech leaves;
That you follow
You may forget.

Oh we remember
We go hence soon
For it is November.

What if it is the tree
Rosaleen and me
Climbed when young –
This the very fork that
First my hand could reach
And then my foot – ah
Such climbings inch by inch:
Look how, one year,
The pruned bark bled.

And in their resting graves,
Our family dead,
Do they sleep aye the deeper,
Knowing we're so sad
Now it's November?

Hansel
for Lawrence and Kate on their wedding day

oak-wood, wild-cherry haulm,
both sides of a blue cloud

star-shavings, wedges of wild-fowl,
ells of snow, blackbird skirls

amethystine tinges, pearly mornings,
the setting of the moon over wild seas

bratticed timber, wood tangles,
cardinal flowers, pini di Roma

one-eyed houses of the poor,
silent music, sounding solitude

chapel-bells, St. John of God,
belonging without knowing

Rosa Mystica, Star of the Sea,
guardian angel, fire-worlds

forty-rod whisky, daws and stars,
whin shags, fairy winds by Slemish

flourishin' curn, pentimento,
Blue Hills of Antrim, Braid Sheddings

Laurentian shores, Glenarm Bay,
The Devenagh Burn, Caugherty

Cliftonville, San Antoine,
brown almonds, rose-red crosses

Carrickfergus, a white-rose of Paradise,
shadows of her hair

amaranthine laurel, day-dawn,
bordures of the silver-shining shield

a thumb-nail's moon, three-tongued islands,
eyes of brown velvet, Santiago

pitch-flavoured wine, brank ursine,
Celtic skies, dream angels

Our Lady of Dreams, Sedes Sapientiae –
the most beautiful Day of the Year so far!

Mistle

She was all chick and churr
constantly repeating herself –
perching on my willow tree,
swaying in the teeth of that gale.

I was hiding under my big oak
wondering about survival,
holding on to thoughts of spring –
would she send me a letter?

The eggs had been laid slowly
– whitish, spotted with reddish and
greyish-brown – in the fork of that tree.
Would they survive?

She's a right old Storm-Cock,
big and fat, her white breast
spotted with dark brown. She's after
snails and slugs, all berries.

I wish I could sing like her,
address her grey-toned plumage.
Though I like fields, gardens and copses
I haven't her teeth.

Hallo, Seághan!

The caravan was handmade, perfect
in every dimension, the blind carpenter
showing it off to the admiring eyes
of the street.
He walked proudly out behind Stuartie
his son, that left hand on his shoulder
as steadying as a gun.
There was a film show running at the time,
deep into the summer of '49.
You could get in for a penny or
a h'penny would do if you knew Patsy
who was giving a talk on 'Pluto & Co.'.
Even if it was only a tea cloth hung up
for a screen we'd never seen anything like it
before, the sawdust spread on the floor
of Herbison's back shed.
We could hear Alec Darragh driving his cow
through the wooden gateway outside,
the tap of his little stick on the side of her rump
an' at the coaxing of her in, we all held our noses
as she let fly on the cribbin.

Andy Milliken was resting his club foot on the kerb
an' watching us kicking an old hairy tennis ball
up against McClintock's gateway.
You're a quare wee dribbler son, he says to me.
You'll make another Charlie McMullan yet,
and I sort of knew to say, *right enough.*

I was wanted by Madge to collect her groceries
an' I ran like a hare from Erwin's with the list,
back along High Street, propping up the heavy
box on the odd window sill 'til I reached Hill Street
by degrees for there was that smell of cookin', an'
the lure of a tanner in my fist.

Francis had called a meeting of his new gang though
we were half in dread of the inside of that old house
an' half afraid of his weird sisters, but went along
for the kick of it when he sent wee Stanley over
to McGroggan's for five Woodbine.
Wilbert had brought cigarette-cards collected
by his uncle Harry in the army and I had my football-
cards of Sam Bartram & Co., but Francis produced
photographs of girls in their bloomers an' we
cleared off up the street towards Devlin's fruit cart.

Mrs Gilmore was washing her kerb, the suds whitening
the step in a half-moon territory, as we dandered on
nonchalantly to raid the applecart but Archie
was pulling a tarpaulin over its back while Stanley
was laughing about the growth of grapes on his ear.
One of the Keenan girls was walking past the shop an'
saying to me quite knowingly, *Hallo, Seághan*, me wondering
who she was addressing, but we had grabbed a few oranges
apiece to run and crawl under the gate of the Baptist
Church and head for the Dispensary.

Wee Stanley tripped over a boot scraper and Mrs McQuitty
spied the oranges flying down the cribbin like
dam-busting bombs but we stuffed them up our jerseys
an' she seemed oblivious anyway since the news was
that Somebody or Other was going to get married.

The caravan was still sitting outside Johnny Herbison's,
even Granny Erwin admiring the windows an'
fine struts along the side, Mary McGoldrick pokin'
her floury head out and Ella at No. 46 had her arms
folded in a smile worthy of a Royal Wedding.

Caugherty FC
for Ferg

i.

The big wicker basket
landed in our hall –
Caugherty FC at rest:
green, deep green,
my father's team.

My mother steeped
each jersey in a metal
tub of boiling water,
adding a kind of soap
left over from the War.

They told me he played
like Stanley Matthews
and I saw him once
at Caugherty, dribbling
up the wing on a Sunday
afternoon. Harryville
Amateurs were after him;
pity he couldn't turn out
of a Saturday – he was
cutting hair 'til it lay
four inches thick on the
cold tiled floor I brushed
and swept like Hercules.

ii.

My father never watched
me play for Antrim; for
Portglenone or the Whitehill;
for Ballymena G.A.C.; for
Queen's or Northern Ireland
Universities; for Eastwood or
Fulwood Amateurs. He never
saw me cut the dribblers down,
– *thou shall not pass,* my motto –
how I got retaliation in first
as a stopper centre half.

iii.

I watch my youngest son
play open-side flanker for
Ireland's Under-19s, admire
his jinking runs, the way he
cuts the centres down. I hear
his trendy travel-bag landing
in our hall and
read again that magic lettering
– what I see is
not Dublin University
Football Club but –
Caugherty F.C.

Doin' the Ton

Great-aunt Mary is one hundred today
though we missed the champagne party,
the birthday card from the Queen, and

her favourite godson, Bertie,
was nowhere to be seen – as
we brought flowers from the city
to Ballycastle Old People's Home.

Great-aunt Mary is one hundred today.

It might have been the sea air,
or the champers on top of the gin
but she was sleeping like a baby
when we walked in.

My three-year-old daughter was frightened by her.
Everybody's nice when they're sleeping,
she said, *but she's very thin.*
(She'd seen her granda lying in his coffin
and she knew this was no fairy).

Mary had her hair done up in a bun
and her rosary beads clutched, like him,
in her left hand. Her skin was
as fresh as milk, her body
like that 'transformed' soul
in heaven that we all wish to become.

Maeve's Great-aunt Mary is one hundred today
and looking very like hersel' –
wouldn't you be frightened
the first time you saw an angel?

N. Antrim

Try standing on tiptoe on this island
looking over at the smaller one
out in the broad Atlantic.

There's magic about the north
of an island, its paths iron underfoot,
its sky closer than the city's
rippling light, its white protection.

The sky is darker in the very northern
corner of a small northern island,
yet there's something tired about a
city twilight, its light too leased.

The northernmost drops of rain,
the jungle of Samhain's shadows,
sound of our bodies near, speak
to our broken hearts.

Tiptoe closer, to the very edge.

Lough Money

'Teach Nead' among the drumlins:
a hiding place for foxes, otters,
an old man's thoughts.

Look at the northern shore –
all business, full of red barns,
soft paths, the planter
touchy about those Christmas trees.

The pike love the bacon, he
told me – a fool casting Swedish
lures across a frozen lough.
I could see a standing stone,
a Church at Saul that Patrick built,
to catch souls, I suppose.

The shock was in catching the fox –
facing me, leaning,
proud and brazen
on the old man's wall.

Ain Toun Bully

Big Tam still stomps along
religiously; likes accusing
hedges, their intimate parts,
of avoiding him, his sham
Irish stare.
There! – in the middle of
the street – *Take it home now
for the missus or her granny.
Shove the berries of this rowan
well up her fanny.*
Suddenly he waxes eloquent:
*Too many red, too many bled;
no a very good sign.*

I reckoned one kick would be
enough under his metal walker
to lay him on his arse in the middle
of Broughshane Road. But I
hesitated for pity – *How sad,
how fresh, the days that are no
more for me* – my god, methought,
time has turned him
into a bit of a poet.

Marengo

I

Marengo, rat-catcher extraordinaire,
christened plain Jean,
lived out his last days
in a small black-slated roof-top apartment
among shrubs from Le Midi, wooden tubs,
occasional Algerian women, Seine barges.

Fourteen years ago, his Caribbean poems
broadcast on Radio Liberty –
each vowel sweetmeat to his cats,
every consonant to the Ciborium of his memory.
One poem, 'Protestant Paris',
appeared in a January *Match*.

II
That very last day, walking through the soft light
of the Rue Rohan to Cluny,
he felt like Pythagoras – among the leaves,
birds and humans, part of the same life.

Our dead are very visible, were his final words,
overheard by a little sad old lady
arranging her lunch on the green park bench.
Bury the leaves yourself, she thought of saying,
but hurried on to find another table for her birds.

Permaculture: Antrim Style
To harm the earth is to heap contempt on the creator,
                                    Chief Seattle, 1854

The Man from Down Under suggested to me
that we should create a hundred villages
to replace any idea of the nation state;
that there was no possibility of a stable
social order without agriculture.

I reminded him that we already have villages.
He said, *Name me one*, and I like a fool
said Broughshane. *But do they practise
permaculture in Broughshane?* he asked.

Well, there's a lot of farmers in The Braid,
I answered, *and they occasionally brave it
into Broughshane.*
Ah there you have it, he said, *what a waste of energy.*

*In a permacultural situation the farmers are the village;
they live in the village as part of nature.*

*Do you mean to tell me that the shops would close down
and Walter Young have to move to Ballymena?*

Correct, he said, *except that Ballymena, obviously
a town, would have to go.*
But I was born in Ballymena, I very foolishly observed,
with some feeling too.
You and the town are part and parcel of the same problem,
the Man said, *and what is more, so is Broughshane.*

Look, I said, *I think Broughshane is not a good starting place. I mean, it's not typical.*
I want everybody in the village to be farmers, he said, and I said most of them had been farmers at one time and had managed to survive through thick and thin.

He wasn't over impressed for his mission was to change a society that was harming itself: he was the boss and had been sent from the World United Federation and proceeded to quote liberally from their handbook.
It was at that point that I lost the bap. *If it hadn't been for St.Patrick, Broughshane might have been a city by now,* I said, *and what does Chief Seattle make of that? I suppose you're looking for a hundred locations to resettle the people in, to harmonise them with nature.*

He looked at me as if I had been a suspect in the Great Grinding or hadn't been reprogrammed in the Final Analysis of '42. I knew there had to be a way to get the bastard off my back and scoomed away on his travels to Worandian.

Only farmers and their families will be permitted to resettle, he said, *the rest to be subject to World Analysis.*
Even I realised what that meant and I didn't fancy much of it for Antrim. Not that such a tiny icrolop of a place would register on their main computage until red alert showed on the giant screens of Westerworld.

I took a chance and poured him a large poitin from Loughguile
in the hope that he would pass over into some other time
or hemiscope. The oul bugger asked me what year I thought it was,
20002? Then he lightened and I told him about St.Patrick
coming down into Broughshane looking for a drink of water and
how at the local well he was told to clear off in no uncertain fashion.
What happened then? he asked, like some schoolchild
that I taught once in Ultissima. *He put a curse on the place*, I said,
slipping him the priest's measure: *Broughshane thou art,
and Broughshane thou wilt be.*

He was having trouble with his metroscan and another dram
had him worrying about explaining his day to That Lot.
He became very amenable to lunch in a local old-fashioned
fast-food restaurant where he could log up notes and pretend
that all was well in old Ultima Thule.

They still spoke in the old tongue in Da Prata's and served
food that could oil one of the ancient carts of Carninny.
I suppose, he asked, *this is typical of the waste in these parts
where the local farmers spend their weekends eating
the produce that they've slaved to grow during the rest of the week?*

You are very well informed, I suggested, *and use more
of the Old Words than most Plancomputels.*

Away or that wae ye, he slurred, *I'm off duty!*

Missing Persons

I would have been listening to British Dance Bands
from the Forties: Lew Stone & His Band,
Ambrose & His Orchestra with Anne Shelton
singing 'Coming In On A Wing and A Prayer';
thinking how my mother played the wireless
endlessly and me sitting in my pram as happy as Larry.
'One of Our Planes is Missing' would have been bad enough
but when Sam Browne sang 'We'll Meet Again'
I would have been jumping out of the pram.

I would have been fuming about half the town being pulled down:
the old school on Ballymoney Street, the Fairhill,
the Manse Wall, High Street, Guy's School,
half of Thomas Street, the Braidwater Mill.

But as the plaintive notes of Lew Stone played on
in my ear I would have been sure it was the people I really missed:
Harry Souters and the fairies in his barrels,
rope sellers, scrap merchants, Bruce and the Millikens
in the Fairhill on a Saturday morning, women in headscarves
in the paisley fashion, dirty bundles of big fivers
coming out of the back pockets of Braid farmers.

But more the families that have gone out of my life:
Erwins, Keenans, Devlins, Balmers. And even more
the particular faces that have passed away: Madge
and Ella, Alec Darragh, Paddy McGroggan, Granny Erwin.

Oh I would have missed the places that have been torn down
but more the faces, their knowing
of my mother, the love of my mother shining
in the old familiar graces of my mother's town.

The Layde, Ballymena
for Anne McAuley

Where is the Layde, my friend, where has it gone?

In those days, the summer sun of the Forties
warm on the legs and the air for breathing
without awareness of the world outside here
along the Layde in the People's Park,
hanging along the low bank, one hand in the cool
shallow stream holding a jam jar, the other
adjusting the belly in position or lapping
the clear water for the fun of it,
was a casual thing to do.

The weed wound the stones and small sticklybacks
easily found the jar and swam around
its perimeter happily enough for a while
until they were emptied back into the stream
at the low bridge near the Park Dam.

In the long evenings there was always a crowd
of youths fishing from the high wall
along by the Devil's Cup and they had fishing rods
and hooks and proper tackle and a good chance
of catching reasonable-sized fish.

Where is the Layde, my friend, where has it gone?

I remember the shock of parking my car on top of
lettuces and cabbages and onions and carrots and
many forgotten leeks and radishes that once grew
happily on the well-tilled soil of the Layde Allotments.

The Layde itself was a stagnant sheugh of a place,
a graveyard for lager cans and rubbish from shopping centres.
The water was dark and streaked with oily patches.
And that was after a period of exile in England and Belfast
and after the Troubles had begun.

The Seventies were a vapour and wasted many's a dream.

While we were sleeping, you and I, Developers
have moved in. I had been sent with a few coppers
to get a big green lettuce full of muck and snails
for the family tea. Now there is an open-air car park,
and smelly ditches like the Layde have been obliterated.
And when I bring my children to show them
where I lazed for sticklybacks they laugh and
think *he's mad as usual about the old days.*

Where has the Layde gone, my friend, where is it now?

Braid Sheddings
for Mark and Margaret

i
The Potato Harvest

A low-backed chariot, wheels spoked
in silvery Antrim morning light
cruised the Rectory Housing Trust Estate.
Fagan's orphans, a motley crew, mixed
in with their peers from Harryville;
Hector's sandy neck barely turning
as he headed his tractor towards the Braid.

Brown earth in waves parting grey
at the back of the valley's head – beautiful
blue spuds culvering up, thrown into Antrim
air-space: halving, quartering – the shining blade
cutting some futures harshly, suddenly, like
heroes of the Somme, autumnal martyrs.

I wanted more and more spuds to appear, to pick
four or five in each hand, to fill the wire basket,
to build up the pit, to take part in the harvest.
The pain in the small of the back was numbed
by the joy of the feel of the spud in the hand,
its tacky clay and sand.

In the middle of the day, the Braid women
brought out enormous baskets of thick sandwiches,
mugs of scaldin' tea: quare packin'!
A girl with lint-white hair and slight turn of eye
looked straight at me, my back against
the chariot wheel, her hot mug cupped
in nervous hands along my thigh. I was shy
and looked away, even from her yellow legs:
thick as pruta-oaten, she would say.

From quiet frontages, respectable windows, the big
Braid houses had humid kitchens full of wholesome
dinners 'til we lined up, stretching to look taller
like soldiers, the drying clay sticking
to the ten bob note that was the warrior's pay.

ii
The Potato Inspector

The year I went with Mark to grade the spuds
I believed the terrible news of the disease
that blighted the life of the farmer's wife and
the death of his brother had me in tears but
The Man from The Ministry chuckled as he skimmed
Craigbilly hedgerows with his Ford all the way home.
He translated the flowers in every field
to Kerr's Pinks, Arran Victors, Chieftains,
Dunbar Standards, Skerry Blues and British Queens.
They also have eyes, Mark said, *tumours and shapes,
but make the flowers your own*; and I thought
of learning Shakespeare off by heart, how P. J. Leahy
would say of *Lycidas* or Hamlet's soliloquy or Keats' *Ode*:
Make it your own, boy. But always I could see
blonde girls from the warm Braid, Marlene or Marilyn
or the flourishin curn that my mother loved
around her mother's doorway, her father's smile.

iii
Peeling Potatoes

In the late Fifties Jimmy Kerr's main duty
was the peeling of the spuds for family dinner
but I was keeping close to him in the kitchen,
waiting 'til he could go with me into our local
jungle. *Jock'll no lay hands on ye. Dinnae
tell me he'll no tak a hint for I'll
bury these clarkes in him tae the thwang holes.* Brian McAuley
and me had been smoking in the Hollow Tree
at a corner of a big field rented by Jock McClelland.
Jock had started to rant and rave at us as we crossed
his potato drills but the more he swore the more
the white blossoms crunched under our feet as we tried
to hop-step and jump over the rigs. We were heart-scared
at his thorn stick and blackened boots and ancient curses.
He was a frightening oul bastard, appearing round
the side of our house, trying to catch sight of me,
swearing about what the police would do, wanting
to humiliate me in front of my parents.
I lay low for weeks and wired Brian to do the same and
the oul bugger faded into the history of growing up.

Brother

From my old bricked-up doorway to the sea,
here, at Marconi's, I can almost touch
The Paps O' Jura.

Rathlin might be a totem pole on its back,
sunk into the North like a low trawler
snailing between the Mull and Benmore.

A hundred webs grow along our outer wall;
the evening sun spotlights their intricate mastery
of swing – supper-time for spiders.

The sea is quiet, just a casual lapping
on Carboniferous; the middle-air secured
by the Rathlin Ferry throbbing home.

Touching may be the simple beauty of the scene
but even this glistening tracery of a hundred
spiders' toil cannot catch the one I miss.

Oh the westering sun signals evening over Moyle
all right but I cannot find the friendly face
I'm looking for even in the water's light.

I am so like the lambent moon,
waiting to see if he appears
round the corner of the Northern Star.

De Natura Rerum

I paint her
                as she sits reading
                Gone With The Wind

It's all hearsay
                she quite suddenly
                reads my thoughts –

this thing about Yeats
                not being buried
                in Drumcliff Churchyard

She sits so still
                she could be a Grimaldi
                in the family waxworks

and I wonder how
                she can read without
                moving her lips.

Paying What They Ask

Sandra was good at making ends meet,
at never eating out, never going on holiday,
at haggling over everything.
She runs my local post office,
just down the road from Belfast Zoo.

Faced with a hooded raider, a couple of
days ago, that wielded a long knife
and a dodgy-looking revolver, together
with a demand for five hundred quid – Sandra
considered the figure: *I can't manage
that*, she said, *how about a tenner and a diet coke?*

Yer man got very annoyed at the haggling
and let off two rounds: one bullet bounced
off the counter and caught in a cornflakes packet;
the other bugger narrowly missed Sandra's left ear
before sinking into a wad of invalidity benefits.

I'll take fifty, the raider rejoined, but Sandra's
partner had sneaked up to whack him on the head
with a packet of frozen peas. *That'll do, James*,
Sandra barked, *the PSNI is on their way. No need
to go to extremes. That fucker 'ud want compensation.*

Headstones
11th Century graveyard at Fröjel, Gotland

This man had been a farmer, Oskar
Krussels from Mulde, a breaker
of earth. This other, a Chief Justice
from Alstade. Nearby, a soldier
and his wife in their family grave.

Here a cottage owner. There
tiny twin headstones for
Helmy Pettersson and her grandson
Olof, aged three: their hearts still close
in little vases, inserts with miniature
roses above a cross-shaped garden.

*Haradsdomare, fanjunkaren, hans maka,
hemmansgaren, landsbrukaren* –
occupations that translate finally
into 'breakers of earth'.
Each, labourer or thinker, farmer
or homemaker, has a tiny star
carved before their birth date, a
simple cross against their death.

Olof is simply 'Olof'. No need
of a surname he hadn't grown into.
Saknad it says on his headstone –
Missed.

The Home Chapel

At that very moment,
along by Carnlough Bay,
Hedgehog spoke to his friend
Blue Robin and the wind blew
over a sea shell, sunlight
penetrated a raindrop.

Hedgehog had a deep desire
to be free of the neon lights
of heaven.
Robin thought that Hedgehog's
hair was too full of tansy, even
bird's foot trefoil:
*That umbelliferous sighing
when you were caught in the
ice storm – that worried me.*

*Your problem is a distinct
lack of camouflage*, Hedgehog
replied.

In the counter twilight
above Glencorp, a greenish-
blue ray, the last to be seen
as the sun dropped below the sea,
entered the raindrop of her eye.

Your real trouble, Robin said,
*is the mist, the transparent blue
veil between your eyes and, well,
everything!*

Wind, sun or rain, old Hedgehog
was last heard to say,
I will not forget her!

2002?

A long time and a short time ago,
in the museum in Wisby,
that man, a Wiking in his armour,
the spitting image of my son.

Fadó – a long time ago –
that came to Ireland in a longboat,
caught a wild trout on a floated worm
at the very mouth of the Quoile.

Long ago in a wild moment
that met the doe-eyed woman.

First Class
Gortgrib 1968

a new school, new classroom, new class –
    but no desks, so we stood looking
    at each other, pretending all
    was as it should be in a new college.

a new school, new classroom, new class –
    but no books, so we headed over
    to the old cabbage patch, pretending
    our coats were goalposts.

a new school, new classroom, new class –
    but no hand bell, so we played
    a massive game of football, pretending
    happiness was on the timetable.

a new school, new mobile, new class –
    but no room under the Christies' desks
    for the awkward legs of my footballers pretending
    they were all still in P7.

a new college, new classroom, new class –
    but no lack of respect for the priest
    as we all stood up, desks attached, pretending
    that Niall held the door for a new President.

The Starry Plough

1

Cold cold my friend
Cold the day
That we buried her in.

Cold through the red clay
In the poor ground
At Milltown.

Cold in the mortuary the evening
Before as we stood round her corpse
And recited the Rosary,

Her beloved Rosary.
Her beloved son standing there
In the Royal Victoria Hospital mortuary.

And he looked at me close
And said in a cold kind of curse:
I'm earning a crust.

They were leering at us,
Cursing our clothes and thinking
Of cars and of accents

But Jesus, didn't she up
Like a cloud and raise herself up
On her elbow

And then up in her shroud altogether
And dandered about to start talking
Aloud of her childhood

How the stars ploughed Dunloy
When she was orphaned at eight,
Said goodbye to her brother at eight.

And everyone there was into
Some prayer and God forgive
But I needed a gin.

I had arrived in the States,
She said, *when they*
Blinded me in

Forced the wrong drops in me eyes
For me sins and what could I do
But return to Big Jim.

And we feared for ourselves for
Neglecting her; crossed ourselves then
In the pain of our sin.

We found a wee house but he drank
His boul self through all
Thick an' thin.

Jesus what is there in life but prayin'
An' weepin' – all of us standing there
Knowing she had been a pious woman

An' thinking holy thoughts
About them poor soldiers walkin' in
An' searchin' roun' the pillows

An' goin' on to raid the whole wee street
though Cape on the Falls was okay
in the days of the mill

when the girls were out workin'
an' payin' for Big Jim ... *but*
it 'ud break the heart of a statue

to talk of the struggle an' that shootin'
by Jim had my oul head rolled in that
never I cared that they'd blinded me in.

2

Grandfather and grandmother McGuckian
and my father's tiny brother Patsy
lay snugly enough where we found them

eventually found them
and the rosary rung over their clay
that cold day of Milltown.

Generations of Irish bones
and intermingled chemicals
and dreams of stars ploughing fields.

Cold the air and cold the clay
that day at Milltown but
surely we thought as the pale sun

scraped our skin
as surely as suffering
has issue

quickened we are thick and thin
from the same red clay
quickened in kin

as surely as the cold
breathes through the clay
in Milltown

green shoots send themselves
through their suffering
to find the light of an Antrim day.

Across Such Great Divide

My first-born son gave me back the sky;
the second carried the spirits of his ancestors.

How Great Thou Art

My youngest son drew raw water from Marconi's well
as if by Providence.
My littlest, my Little Dorrit, so like her mother
across the eyes, dances and laughs and pirouettes
just like my own mother.

How Great Thou Art

When Seághan Quixote meets his Maker
he might say in all humility,
Oh how very much like me they were, or
How much they take after their father.

Across Such Great Divide –
How Great Thou Art.

Midlands

Light buoyant in Kilbeggan,
Tyrellspass,
Everywhere in my own country.

Still evening over Shannon,
Lough Ennel not too far away,
Cnoc Buadha close.

How I miss that other life
I might have had,
This little G.A.A. ground,

The 'village' team called
'Clan na Gael',
The 'heathen games'

We played at Caugherty
Lost in a suffering mist
Swept over Slemish.

The Last Pair of Wolves

Aughnabrack, 1692

Hunger drove her out beyond our wood,
and she made her water on a nettle-bank
but sank again into a deeper mood,
the countryside being plentiless and dank.

We can breathe more easily apart –
her teeth like almonds large and white and bare,
into the very centre of my heart
that dart – and mount her then I could not dare.

That very day they'd meant to kill us both
and I left my favourite Antrim hill alone
– ten years ago today since we'd been troth –
heard a little crack, a whistle on her bone.

Together we had already died.
Apart my love, can I live on? I cried.

Alone

Wolf could see a steading and its fold,
but tired and sick of footprints of their kind
he turned and missed the company of old –
stoats not chickens roosting in his mind.

The dense sweet sudden twittering of elves,
a hiddenness beneath a bosky brae,
sent him backwards into olden delves,
the slaethorn of his father's day.

He vanished into places once his own:
Dunaghy, Doagh, fair Antrim, and old Slaght
of younger days when he was not alone –
along the Braid, flax reeds his bedded mat.

All he had was the amber of her eyes,
a memory of flowering weeds her sighs.

Breath Across the Braid
in memoriam Henry McAuley

wind sharpening
in the sighing of tall trees
above the graves

made her turn
sighing
to Caugherty

a scythe sharpening
in the Slemish wind
made her turn

the infant leapt
in her womb
to the sighing

from the Pillars
a breath across the Braid
made her turn

her father's voice
sweet as buttermilk
made her turn

from the day's
foul factory air
a tune of memory

a riddle from Crebilly
Castle, a corncrake
in the Deerfin moss

they collected clouds
ate raw turnips from
a cousin's field

from his inside pocket
a tin whistle
to a note of 'C'

scuffed shadows sent
like mice
to the nearest friendly door

White Rainbow
Though seas between us braid ha' roared,
                                        Burns

She seems so far away,
even from The Plough,
Kintyre's long eye.

She seems remote,
even from Tornaroan,
the Sea of Moyle.

She seems so distant,
even from the Benmore moon,
the Paps O' Jura.

Death removed her charms
even from Carey,
the Blue Arms of Antrim.

The Effect of Lightning
Saint Catherine of Siena

I knelt for the lovely stone
as often as any man,
but this was different, this
tree of death.

Two branches of her little body
lay greying, below, behind bars
in a casket of gold. Remodelled,
her head sat on the altar, in Siena.
The rest of her, elsewhere.

The Yew loves cliff-faces,
shade-tolerant, beyond grazing,
but the effect of lightning makes
weeping trees – like scale bark
it broke off in broad flat flakes
so that there was no original skin
on her face.

They said that it had been medieval,
the fire, her mortal face beyond repair;
a page ripped out of a manuscript,
there, on her tree of death.

Such a tiny figure of a girl, water
to bone – why gird her with gold and silver?
I knelt at the *prie-dieu* as often
as any man – but this was different.

At home, in Antrim, the July day full
of thunder and lightning, broad flat flakes
of dangerous skin fell off my head
in scale bark, and I wept like a tree.
Should I report this, I said, *to – to
the authorities?*

Gonzalo de Cordoba – The Great Captain
for Brian

He liked the sounds of air,
tones of it:
in the hollow china insulators supporting the wires;
wind blowing over a sea shell
pronouncing a high pitch; or its low-pitched howl
striking the opening of a cave.

In still air he could hear
earth-rumblings, their origin in the depths,
in the dying-down of distant earthquakes.

He could hear robins crying,
knew they were dying in their desire to be free.

When swifts or swallows flew over an ancient wall
he heard them flying madly over heaven,
quivering like wildflowers in a quag.

Of course, he had to have a house by the sea:
the waves that threatened some were his security;
the tide sucking Carboniferous pebbles, his infancy.

He knew the very river breathed the sea-filled air,
that it wanted to become a babbling brook
by drawing air beneath itself
only to release it fully free again.

Matamoros

Maria Jesus Lorenzo Modia
fed me words in Galego:
for my homesickness *'morriña'*,
'orballo' for Belfast's soft rain.
*Your Antrim is like Buenos Aires,
the Fifth Province of Galicia.*

Maria Jesus Lorenzo Modia
flew her baby Merc at ninety
from La Corunna to the twin spires
of Santiago as I prayed little words
in Gaeilge to reduce her speed.

Maria Jesus Lorenzo Modia's
favourite blue plastic rosaries
clung tight round her mirror
like Charlie Agnew's Lourdes
magnet kept his Beetle safe
between Glenariff and Glenarm.

Maria Jesus Lorenzo Modia's
father fought for Franco and
left her a farm near Lugo that
flashed past so quickly she
hadn't time to renovate it.

Maria Jesus Lorenzo Modia,
fed Castilian words by her mother
for modernity, for a career, felt like
a poor Gaelic scholar in Galway
wearing the English halter for progress.

Mari Jesus Lorenzo Modia
found us the tomb of San Jacobi,
altars of San Antonio, beautiful Gemma,
the great thurible of de Compostela.
It may be Priscillian in the silver casket
but does it matter – he's ours.

Maria Jesus Lorenzo Modia's
family took us to the Opus Dei school
sports, watched their littlest run like
an Irish hare past the tomb of Sir John Moore.
O'Mahony and O'Neill came here: look
at the gentle faces of ancient Ireland.

Maria Jesus Lorenzo Modia
followed us and her son up the steps
of the Lighthouse of Hercules, the Celtic
Nations amassed round its Roman foundations,
and Mici Sheáin O'Neill's words beaconed:
Is Gaeil sinn agus is Gaeil ár sinsir
leis na mílte bliain anall.

Maria Jesus Lorenzo Modia
flew her baby Merc on the return journey
at a hundred for all I cared, armed as
I was with the sword of St. James, his shield
and white horse. Oh I killed Moors all the way
back from Galicia to Galgorm!

The Tao of Pooh
for Bella

Apparently, according to SOMEONE,
there was only three-quarters of the sky left.
You couldn't possibly lower a sail
near the shore – clouds were falling everywhere!

Pooh was looking in his left pocket
for something. Rabbit asked him what
could ever patch the sky. *Better to ask
Owl*, thought Eyeore, *because Knowledge
might do it.*

Piglet was home again with the news
that the sky had caught fire. SOMEONE
had said that there might have to be
a New Glass Sky.

What will happen to the stars? asked Owl.
If only SOMEONE had time in their pocket.
What possible use could Time be? asked rabbit,
if SOMEONE had stolen a bit of the sky.

How could anyone be so foolish? said Owl.
*Shadows will have to be hung up, the river
will lose its gleam.*

Let's go and see Christopher Robin, said Pooh,
*for a little something, as soon as possible,
since it's Thursday.*

Christopher Robin agreed that the sky
appeared quite lonely, like a moth
hung upside down in an old barn.

Pooh said it was a fine day for a little turn
along the river and a honey jar might help.
What have you got in your pocket?
asked Christopher Robin.

Soft patches of Clear Glow, said Pooh,
and a swarm of bees!

Geography Lessons

Ballymena Technical College, 1968
for Liam Neeson

When I strolled in,
he was entertaining 3C:
strutting the boards, front-stage,
showing off my graduation gown,
gesticulating, doing *The Duke*, happy.

I says, *Liam, you're a born actor!* –
my one claim to fame.

St Patrick's College, 1982
for Anthony Kelly, Form 2A, tragically killed on his bicycle

In our geography of dreams
he was a quark: his flinted smile;
climbing the side of the house
like a Masquerade.

Pure joy of life grew
through his spider-catching eyes.

In the alchemy of his ways he could run
with the gypsies through the tails
of a nettle garden, making gold out of sorrow,
a springing year into a litany of steps.

There he is at the front of my class, smiling
Dare you, Duke, to cycle across!

Ballymena Sky

Moon in a golden field,
handclasp of winter and spring,
the warring wind.

Tendrils of woodbine
over a white gate,
the evening star.

A daffodil light
for sparrows of the old town
in a night-wind.

Across the valley of the Braid
a strong angel of great pity –
the earth a shadow of heaven.

Our own Ballymena moon is high
as the Lord of this mansion of life –
an hour across the Waters of Remembrance!

Shadows of ourselves
in his gentleness, his tenderness,
down the Sheddings towards home!